HOW THEY MADE THINGS WORK!
THE EGYPTIANS

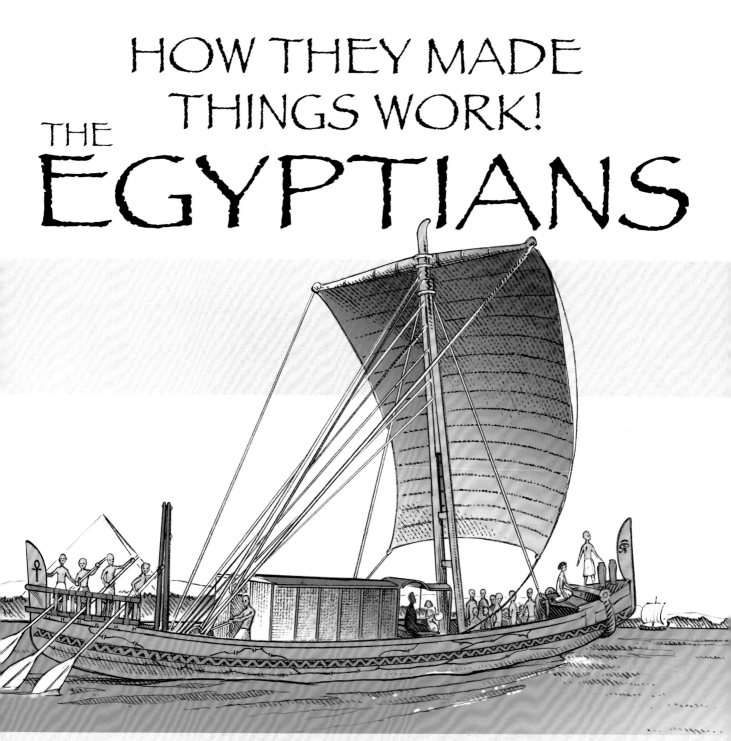

Written by Richard Platt • Illustrated by David Lawrence

W

FRANKLIN WATTS
LONDON • SYDNEY

First published in 2008 by Franklin Watts

Franklin Watts
338 Euston Road
London NW1 3BH

Franklin Watts Australia
Level 17/207 Kent Street
Sydney NSW 2000

A CIP catalogue record is available from the British Library.

Dewey number: 609

ISBN 978 0 7496 7477 9

Printed in China

Franklin Watts is a division of Hachette Children's Books, an Hachette Livre UK company.
www.hachettelivre.co.uk

Editor in Chief John C. Miles
Editor Sarah Ridley
Art Director Jonathan Hair
Designers Rachel Hamdi and Holly Fulbrook
Picture research Sarah Smithies

Contents

HOW THE EGYPTIANS MADE THINGS WORK

On the moist, muddy banks of the River Nile, the people of ancient Egypt farmed and prospered. Around 5,000 years ago, they began to build a remarkably modern way of life. They created great cities, and amazing tombs and temples. They wrote down their language and measured time with clocks and calendars.

Controlling mud and water

The ingenious Egyptians were a practical people. Many of their inventions were connected with their precious river and the farming it made possible. They learned to trap and raise its waters to grow their crops taller. They developed sailing ships to travel quickly up and down the Nile. And they tilled Egypt's black mud with ploughs pulled by cattle. They even learned to measure the height of the Nile's floodwaters. They used this information to predict the harvest – and set the taxes for the next year!

Temples and pyramids

However, Egyptians did not use science and technology just for practical reasons. A lot of their inventions aimed to glorify gods, kings and the dead. Though they lived in mud-brick houses, they cut and hauled huge stone blocks to build palaces and pyramids. Within stone temples, priests watched the stars, timing their movement to plan their prayers. The deeply religious Egyptian people found ways to preserve dead bodies, believing people would live again after they had died.

Egypt's dry climate stopped workers' tools, kings' treasures and scribes' writings from rotting away to dust. Today, these objects tell a remarkable story of an ancient people who used their skills to make life easier and richer.

EMBALMING

An Egyptian priest sets to work in the scorching desert. Whispering a sacred spell, he pushes an iron hook up the nose of a stinky dead body and scrapes out the brains. This is the first stage of making a mummy. When it's complete, in ten weeks' time, the dead man will look almost as fresh as the day he died – and stay that way forever.

> **Hello, Mummy!**

Stop the rot!

Egyptian people believed that when they died they could live again, in the afterlife. However, this would happen only if they had the right funeral, with special tomb equipment and statues. And most important of all, they could not enjoy eternal life if their bodies rotted.

How to make a mummy

Don't try this at home! Mummification only works if you also chant the right secret prayers.

1 Brains out

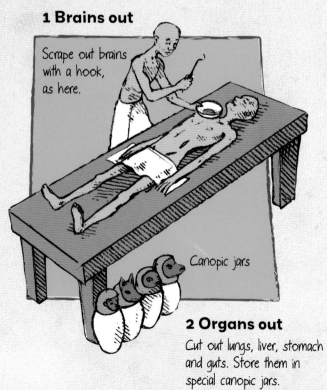

Scrape out brains with a hook, as here.

Canopic jars

2 Organs out

Cut out lungs, liver, stomach and guts. Store them in special canopic jars.

3 Clean up

Wash the body inside and out with palm wine and spices.

Natron

4 Dry out

Bury the body in natron – a mineral salt. For an adult you'll need 180 kg (400 lb).

Mummy magic

Egypt's hot sands suck the moisture from buried bodies, slowing their decay. From about 5,000 years ago, Egyptian people began to improve on nature. They used preservative salts, resin and spices, and they wrapped the corpse in cloth. Pickled like this, some mummies survive to the present day.

Canopic jars

The insides of the dead were stored in special canopic jars. Gods carved on the stoppers guarded each jar's contents.

5 Resin and bandages on

After ten weeks, remove from natron, cover in resin and wrap in linen strips.

Egyptians believed the jackal-headed god Anubis took care of mummies in the afterlife. Priests wore Anubis masks to carry out some of the rituals of mummification.

6 Into a coffin

Store mummy in a sarcophagus (stone coffin) painted with a picture of the deceased.

Laid flat, the linen used to wrap a top-class mummy would cover three tennis courts.

Sometimes priests covered the mummy's head and shoulders with a mask made of papier-maché, and painted with the dead person's portrait, before putting it in the sarcophagus.

Everlasting cat

Sacred animals got the mummification treatment, too, like the cat above. In Egyptian tombs archaeologists have found mummies of snakes, birds, lizards, dogs, gazelles, rams – even an egg.

7 Into the tomb

Bury in a tunnel cut into desert rock, or under a huge triangular thingey. Your choice. That's it.

It's all about floods.

IRRIGATION

In a dusty valley some 30 km (20 miles) from Cairo, Egypt's capital, is a crumbling wall called Sadd-el-Kafara. It is all that remains of one of the ancient Egyptians' greatest inventions: a dam. With the help of canals, ditches, embankments and dams like Sadd-el-Kafara, Egyptians tamed the flooding waters of the River Nile. They turned the Sahara desert into green farmland.

Crop crisis

Each year the River Nile rose, flooding the surrounding land. When the river level fell again, Egypt's farmers were able to grow crops in the rich mud left behind. Soon, though, the Nile valley dried out. For half the year the desert sun baked the rich, fertile mud iron-hard, and crops withered.

Irrigation

By irrigating (watering) their fields, Egyptian farmers doubled their harvests. They built dykes (earth walls) to keep their fields wet when the flood-waters fell. In the dry season, they used bucket-lifting machines, such as the shaduf, to raise the water to their fields.

Floods and fields

On the flat land on either side of the river, farmers raised dykes up to 2 m (6.5 ft) high. They divided the land into huge rectangular basins. The biggest was the size of 20,000 football pitches. At flood time the Nile water turned these fields into lakes.

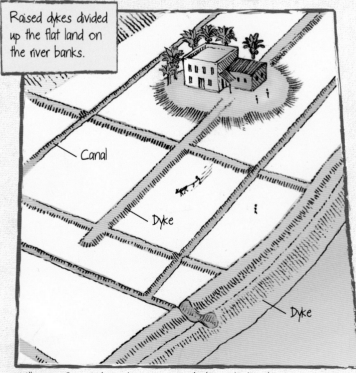

Raised dykes divided up the flat land on the river banks.

Canal

Dyke

Dyke

Villages of mud-brick houses were built on higher land.

Shaduf

Raising water is back-breaking work. Egyptian farmers made it easier with the shaduf. Palm-trunk columns supported a swinging pole. At one end was a bucket on a rope. A weight at the other end balanced a full bucket. Pulling the arm down to fill the bucket was much less tiring than lifting the bucket to tip water into a canal.

When the river flooded, water flowed into the basins through openings in the dykes.

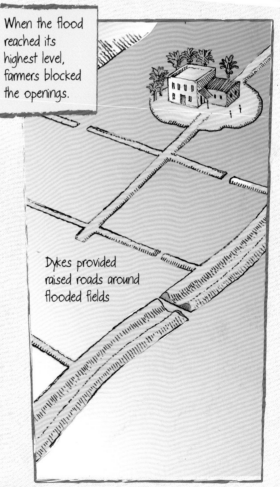

When the flood reached its highest level, farmers blocked the openings.

Dykes provided raised roads around flooded fields

Water flowing into field

Main river channel

Canals carried some of the water out to areas that the flood did not reach.

When the land was thoroughly soaked a month later, the gaps were opened again. Irrigation made possible several harvests each year.

ASTRONOMY AND TIME

To the Egyptian peasant working in a muddy field, the time of day hardly mattered: he laboured until his work was done. To the priests, though, knowing the time was vital. Temple life ran on a timetable as regular as a modern railway schedule. Without mechanical clocks, priests told the time by measuring the movement of the sun and stars.

Counting the hours

Egyptians believed in dozens of gods. They worshipped them in rituals (religious services) that they thought controlled the weather, the harvests, and everything else in life. Temple priests needed to count the hours so that they prayed to each god at the correct time every day.

Priest astronomers

To measure time, priests watched how the sun moved across the sky and made the first shadow clocks from stone. When the sun set, they measured the movement of the stars, using a "merkhet" instrument with a stretched cord, and a split palm leaf.

Sun clock

In the morning, priests placed clocks like the one shown left with the end block towards the rising sun. As the sun rose higher in the sky, the shadow of the block grew shorter. Marks on the base showed the length of the shadow at each of five hours in the morning. When the sun was overhead the shadow disappeared, and the priests turned the clock around. The sinking sun made the shadow cross the marks once again, thus counting the hours of the afternoon.

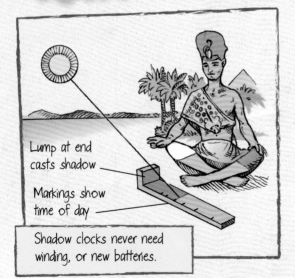

Lump at end casts shadow

Markings show time of day

Shadow clocks never need winding, or new batteries.

Dripping time

Egyptian priests also used water clocks, or clepsydras, to measure time at night. They filled a stone tub with water, and watched the level fall as the water flowed out through a small hole near the bottom. Lines inside marked the water level at each hour.

Stargazers

When the sun had set, the priests used the movement of the stars to count the hours. Looking West, they took careful note of which constellations were setting, then found the time from charts. The times when stars set slowly change through the year, so the priests used 36 tables, one for each decan (ten days).

"Merkhet" instrument

Split palm leaf

Merkhet instrument held weighted cord

Split palm leaf used for sighting

Roof of temple

GLASS

Anyone for a beach barbecue?

Today glass is cheap and common. We pour and sip drinks from containers made of it, and look straight through it in windows. However, to Egyptians 5,000 years ago glass was precious and scarce. They coloured it blue and used it like jewels. More than a thousand years passed before Egyptians learned to make simple glass containers.

Early glass

It's possible to make glass just by heating sand, but you need a very hot fire. So the first Egyptian glass was really a glaze – a shiny coating on stone or pottery. Called faience, this blue material was strong enough to make into small ornaments. Real glass probably wasn't possible until some Egyptians had a barbecue on the beach.

Invention or accident?

Mixing sand with a chemical called soda ash allowed Egyptians to make glass in cooler fires. Soda ash comes from burned seaweed, so the invention of glass may have followed a seaside fire. The invention of glass probably happened on an Egyptian beach, or one in Mesopotamia – what is now Syria, Iraq and Turkey.

Making a glass vessel

Glassmakers first collected chalk, sand and the ash of seaweed, or the saltmarsh plant glasswort.

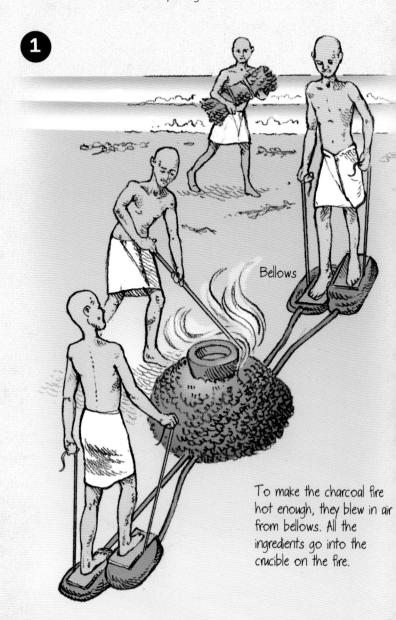

Bellows

To make the charcoal fire hot enough, they blew in air from bellows. All the ingredients go into the crucible on the fire.

What happened next?

Simple glass made of seaweed and sand is not much use because water dissolves it. Egyptian glassmakers solved this problem by adding chalk. Later they made containers by coating lumps of clay with glass. Scraping out the clay when the glass was cool created bottles.

See-through stone

Egyptian craftsmen made bottles and vases without glass by carving them from stone. Using copper drills, they ground the stone so thin that light shone through it.

2

A glassmaker filled a bag with a mixture of clay and sand.

3

He stuck a metal rod into the bag and dipped it quickly into the molten glass. Later, he removed the rod and shook out the bag of clay and sand from the glass vessel.

Fish bottle

Glassmakers in Egypt were so skilled that by 1350 BCE they were creating brilliantly-coloured glass containers, like this fish. It may have been the work of a foreign artist. Egypt had powerful armies and in wars with its northern neighbours, they captured and enslaved foreign craftsmen.

STONE WORKING

We need some rock music to work to.

Few trees grow in Egypt's desert climate, so wood was always scarce and costly. In place of timber, ancient Egyptians used rock for their most important buildings. In huge quarries they cut enormous blocks of stone completely by hand. They moved the blocks – often over vast distances – without using wheeled vehicles.

Hard work for masons

Rock is hard and heavy! Cutting it takes a lot of effort, even with the sharp power tools we have today. There's more work to be done once a stone block is cut; moving it is a sweaty, gruelling effort, especially in Egypt's hot sun. Wheels would have made the job easier but none were strong enough to support heavy weights.

Banging wedges into a crack.

Pouring water on wooden wedges.

Ooops!

Egyptian masons (stone workers) sometimes had failures. This huge obelisk at Aswan – 42 m (138 ft) long – cracked before it could be chipped out of the quarry. Studying its sides has helped archaeologists guess how masons cut stone.

Extracting stone

The chisels, drills and saws Egyptian masons used were made from copper. This metal is 150 times softer than the diamond-tipped tools in use today. So in a quarry, masons hammered the rock with hard stone balls. This chipped away a wide groove separating the blocks from the hillside. They split out the blocks by banging in wooden wedges. Soaked in water, the wood swelled, cracking the stone.

Massive ships

The huge barges used to carry obelisks down the River Nile were as long as football pitches. No bigger ships were built for 3,300 years.

Stone barge

Quarry is near river bank

Sledge with stone block

Wooden wedges

Moving the rock

Masons used sledges to shift the heavy blocks. Thousands of them pulled on ropes tied to the sledges. They poured water or oil onto the runners to make them slip along. To move stone long distances they loaded it onto enormous barges. A barge took a month to carry stone the length of the country. The River Nile was Egypt's highway.

Stone balls

PYRAMIDS

Towering high above Egypt's capital, pharaoh Khufu's Great Pyramid is the world's biggest tombstone. Its massive size has astonished visitors ever since it was finished, some 4,500 years ago. To construct this and other huge monuments, as many as one in six of the country's people became builders.

What an effort!

Egyptians believed that they could live again after death – but only if their preserved bodies were not damaged. For about 1,000 years Egypt's pharaohs built pyramids to protect their mummies. Constructing these vast tombs required careful measurements, a huge workforce and clever organization.

Keeping the farmers busy

Each year the River Nile rose, flooding the land and stopping farm work. The pharaoh employed farmers as builders while their land dried. To build the Great Pyramid, they cut 2.5 million stone blocks weighing up to 70 tonnes each, and lifted some as high as a 40-storey building. A small army of officials tracked progress, and kept workers fed and paid.

The Nile flooded its river valley for about two months each summer. The high water level allowed vast stone barges to sail from Aswan, 900 km (550 miles) to present-day Cairo.

Workers hauled stone in teams, probably up ramps winding round the sides.

Most stone blocks weighed about 2.5 tonnes – as much as a 4 x 4 (SUV) car.

Miaow to the max!

The Great Pyramid still stands, guarded by the Sphinx, a massive stone sculpture that's half-cat and half-human.

To complete the pyramid in 20 years, workers had to lay a block every two minutes.

Besides wages, workers got a supply of food – mostly bread, fish, vegetables, dates and beer – clothes and pots.

Workers quarried most of the stone for the pyramid nearby.

A walk out

In 1158 BCE men building the tomb of Ramesses III went on strike because they had run short of food and of the black make-up they used to protect their eyes from the sun's glare.

SAILING SHIPS

The River Nile provided Egypt's people with a transport superhighway. On the simplest of boats they could drift north from Nubia to the Mediterranean Sea 1,000 km (600 miles) away. With the invention of the sail they could travel the other way almost as easily.

Travel troubles

Travelling any distance through Egypt's long, thin land meant a boat journey. Nile boatmen could rest on their oars while drifting downstream. However, to travel south, they had to row against the current. To make things worse, wooden boats were hard to build because Egypt's small trees became short planks. Most boats were made of reed bundles.

When the wind blows from behind, as on the Nile, a mast at the front works well. But when Nile boatmen began to sail downstream, they had to move the mast to the middle.

Crew lowered mast when it was not needed, resting it on a pole-like stand.

Stem

Reed boat

Egyptian hunters made one-man rafts no bigger than surfboards by tying together in small bundles the reeds that grew abundantly along the Nile banks. Making boats just meant binding bigger bundles and more of them. Even when Egyptian boat builders began to use wood, they curved up the fronts and backs of their ships to imitate the shape of traditional reed craft (above).

Crew steered the boat using oars.

Sail solution

Egypt's winds blow from the north. Nile boatmen discovered that if they spread sheets of cloth above their boats, the steady breeze would give them a free ride south. They got round the shortage of wood by using rope to stitch short planks together and make bigger ships.

Two-legged mast

A single mast would have put too much strain on a reed hull, so boats had twin masts.

This is a river ship. Ocean-going ships were made stronger with a rope that went all the way from the bows to the stern.

Sail made from linen or from matting.

Mast cross-bars formed ladder.

Bow

OX-DRAWN PLOUGHS

It was Egypt's hard-working farmers who made possible the rich society that flourished in the Nile valley. The grain and other crops they grew fed priests and scribes who did no work on the land. But Egypt's big harvests would have been impossible without ploughs.

No bull, honest!

Mud and misery

Grain grew tall and fast from the sticky mud left by the Nile floods, but tilling this black soil was exhausting. In ancient times, farmers planted seeds in furrows cut by crude hoes: forked sticks tipped with stone. Farmers may have worked in pairs. One kept the hoe upright and the other pulled it with a rope. But even with team-work, farmers could not cultivate all the fertile land along the Nile banks.

The clever farmer

At some time before the start of the Old Kingdom (2700 BCE), a clever (or lazy) farmer hit upon the idea of hitching the hoe to an ox (bull), creating what we now call a plough. Far stronger than a man, an ox could plough much bigger areas. Egyptian agriculture spread to fill the whole Nile valley.

Farming in ancient Egypt - from a wall painting

Flooding covered the field in black silt. This shows hoeing.

Ploughing dug a groove in the soft mud.

Sowing seed – most was scattered, but flax was dropped into the furrow so that it grew in rows.

Ox ploughs today

For Egyptian farms smaller than about 50 hectares (125 acres), ploughing and other farm work with oxen is still better than using a tractor. Oxen are cheap to feed and don't need oil, repairs or insurance. You can still see them at work in fields along the Nile.

Ox-plough at work

Egyptian farmers tied the horns of two oxen to a strong timber yoke and fixed the pole of the plough to it. The farmer walked behind, guiding the plough blade and keeping it at just the right depth.

Sowing seeds.

Driving beasts over the soil trod the seed in.

Carrying the harvest home.

Picking up fallen grain.

Harvesting using flint-edged sickles.

Take a letter!

PAPER AND INK

Organizing Egypt's land, people, crops and taxes would have been impossible without writing. Men who could write were called scribes. Their skill made them powerful and wealthy. Egyptian scribes were not the first people to write, but they invented three new tools to make it easier: pen, ink and paper. Nobody thought of a better way of writing until the invention of the typewriter some 4,000 years later.

Record keeping

Egyptian farmers gave their rulers some of the grain they grew as taxes. But how much should they pay? To make a fair decision, scribes needed to keep records of farm and field sizes, and how high the Nile flood rose (see page 24). In neighbouring countries scribes pressed writing into soft clay blocks, but this created bulky, heavy records.

This beautiful statue depicting a sitting scribe was made in about 3500 BCE.

Reeding and writing

Some time before 2300 BCE scribes had begun using Nile reeds to make both pen and paper. Chewing or cutting the end of a reed turned it into a brush or nib. By flattening and joining the reed's soft core they created papyrus – a sheet or scroll much like paper. They made ink by pounding soot with sticky plant gum.

Making papyrus

 1 Cut off the outside of the wet reed and cut slices from the pithy middle.

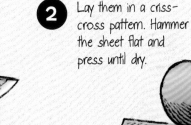 **2** Lay them in a criss-cross pattern. Hammer the sheet flat and press until dry.

3 When dry, rub the ridges off with a polished stone.

Hieroglyphic writing

At first scribes used picture writing, drawing walking legs, for example, to spell "movement". For words that were impossible to draw they sometimes combined objects with similar sounds. Drawing a bee and a leaf, for instance, spells "belief". To make writing quicker scribes eventually arranged 24 signs into an alphabet. A foot, for instance, spelled "B"; a snake was a letter "J".

A B D F G H I J K M N P R S T W Y

MEASUREMENTS

Ancient Egypt was a land shaped like a rope, and for the surveyors who measured it, a knotted rope was the most important tool. They used it to put back field boundaries after the Nile floods, and to lay out new buildings. The rope wasn't the only measuring tool, though: Egyptians used accurate rulers and scales, and invented the set-square for setting out right-angles.

A knotty problem.

It WAS there, honest!

For a couple of months of the year, the Nile floods hid farmland. When the water went down, mud covered the field boundaries. Farmers marked the corners of their fields with stones, but greedy neighbours could move these to steal land. Who could sort these problems out?

Measuring men

Scribes measured the fields with ropes, to settle who owned what – and how much tax they should pay! They measured shorter distances with units based on the human body. Surveyor-scribes also made maps and helped set out the foundations of buildings. They used the positions of the stars to make sure temples faced exactly the right way.

Stretching a rope

Egyptians called surveyors "rope stretchers", for this is just what they did. In the scene below, copied from the Luxor tomb of Menna, Scribe of the Fields, three surveyors pull tight their knotted measuring rope to judge the length of the corn field behind.

Regularly spaced knots show how much rope surveyor-scribes have unrolled.

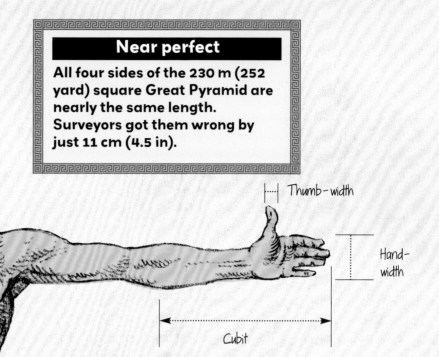

Near perfect

All four sides of the 230 m (252 yard) square Great Pyramid are nearly the same length. Surveyors got them wrong by just 11 cm (4.5 in).

Thumb-width

Hand-width

Cubit

Measuring length

The most common and useful unit of length was the cubit, the distance from the elbow to the tip of the middle finger, or 52 cm (20 in). The hieroglyph (written form) of a cubit was an outstretched arm. Egyptians measured smaller things with the foot (half a cubit), a hand-width (a seventh of a cubit) and a thumb-width (a quarter of a hand-width). Longer units, for surveying, were the meh-ta of 100 cubits.

Weights

The first use of a balance in Egypt was for weighing gold. Early balances were made of limestone, with limestone weights. Some later weights were shaped like animals, such as this hippopotamus.

Like my designer frock?

LOOMS

Wealthy Egyptians were snappy dressers! Women and men wore kilts made from finely-woven linen, pressed in neat pleats (side-by-side creases). To stay cool in Egypt's desert climate, some of their clothes were see-through thin. Fine fabrics like these were made possible by the invention of the loom (weaving frame).

Cool clothes

Egypt's fierce sunshine tans and wrinkles skin. Desert nights are as cold as the days are hot. Going naked was uncomfortable, and animal-skin clothes too thick for the day-time heat. Egyptian men also admired untanned women: tomb paintings show wives much paler than husbands.

Inventing the loom

Some time before 5000 BCE ingenious Egyptians had learned to stretch rows of threads side-by-side (the warp). They made fabric by pulling across them more threads (the weft) in an over-under-over-under pattern. Called weaving, this process probably began on the ground. Four pegs hammered into the earth held the two poles around which the weaver wound the warp threads. This simple frame was the first loom. The weaver wound the weft thread onto a wooden strip called a shuttle to pass it through the loom.

Shuttle

Weft

Warp

Shed-rod   Heddle

Craft weaver

Nubian craft workers in Egypt still weave brilliantly-coloured cloth on looms that have not changed design in 4,000 years.

Finest fabric

Lengths of the finest Egyptian fabric were so thin that they could be pulled through a finger ring.

Ground loom

To make a fabric's criss-cross pattern, weavers must first lift, then lower every other warp thread. From about 2000 BCE they did this with a heddle – a rod tied to alternate threads. Twisting a flat strip of wood called a shed-rod flipped from over to under.

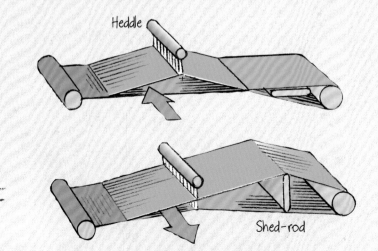

Heddle

Shed-rod

Body lice evidence

Though the oldest clothes have not survived we know that people stopped going about naked at least 30,000 years ago, because body lice (which live only in clothes) had evolved before this.

MIRRORS AND COSMETICS

The Egyptians did not invent vanity: even the earliest humans must have admired their own reflections in still pools of water. But the Egyptians did mix the world's first cosmetics, and polished up metal discs to make mirrors that they could hold in their hands.

Health problems

We don't know for sure why Egyptians first made make-up but it may have been to cure eye and skin problems. Brilliant sunlight is dazzling. It can cause eyestrain and – at worst – blinding cataracts. Egypt's hot climate also dries the skin, and encourages the spread of insects and diseases that irritate the eyes.

Early cosmetics

Men and women painted their faces – and especially their eyes (right) – with coloured ointments that we would now call cosmetics. Men used a black eye ointment called mesdemet, which was made from minerals ground up with animal fat. These cut the sun's glare. Women used colour, painting blue or green around their eyes, eyelids and brows.

This wall-painting shows ancient Egyptian women applying make-up.

Medical make-up

The bright blues and greens of Egyptian make-up came from copper minerals. Recent medical research has shown that these can kill germs. The minerals in black make-up were disinfectants and kept flies away. So painting eyes may have kept them healthy, too.

Checking the mirror

The first Egyptian mirrors may have been made of smooth stone. Soaked in water, these were briefly reflective but soon turned dull as they dried. Mirrors made of bronze – a mixture of copper and tin metals – were in use by about 3200 BCE (left). Polished to a high shine, they worked well.

GLOSSARY

afterlife New, better life in which Egyptians believed the dead could live again, as long as they were buried correctly.

astronomer Someone who studies the stars.

canopic jar Special jar used to store the organs removed from a mummy.

chalk Soft white rock used for making glass.

clay Fine mud that is soft and easily shaped when wet, yet hard when dry.

constellation Group of stars in the sky, often named by ASTRONOMERS after objects their arrangement resembles.

copper Soft, orange-coloured metal that is easily shaped into tools or weapons.

corpse Dead body, usually of a human.

cosmetics Make-up.

crop Plant grown to eat, or to feed to animals.

fertile Soil containing the goodness that plants need to grow well.

furrow Groove cut in farm land, often by a PLOUGH, for planting CROPS.

glaze Shiny, glass-like coating often added to pottery to decorate it or make it waterproof.

heddle Part of a LOOM that lifts the WARP threads so that the SHUTTLE can WEAVE the over-under-over pattern that holds fabric together.

hoe Farm tool used for weeding and to TILL soil.

irrigate To water CROPS so that they grow better.

kilt Skirt worn by men.

lice Tiny bugs that cling to humans and animals, feeding on blood, skin and sweat.

limestone White or pale rock often used as a building material.

loom Frame used for WEAVING threads in a criss-cross pattern to make them into cloth.

natron Chemical used to preserve a mummy; a natural mixture of baking powder and washing soda.

nib Writing tip of a pen.

oar Pole with a wide flat end that is pulled through water to move a boat along.

obelisk Tall, thin, pointy, four-sided pillar of stone used to mark a special place.

ointment Medical paste rubbed on the skin to soothe or heal.

ox Cow or bull often used to pull a cart or PLOUGH.

papyrus Paper-like writing material made from the spongy middle of marsh reeds.

pleats Rows of decorative creases deliberately pressed into clothes.

plough Farm tool, usually pulled by animals, to turn over soil and dig a FURROW.

pyramid Object with a wide base, a pointed top, and TRIANGLE-shaped sides.

quarry Place where building stone is dug from the ground.

resin Soft or liquid plastic-like material that sets hard.

right-angle The angle formed when a circle is divided exactly into four equal quarters; or the angle between flat, level ground and anything standing exactly upright.

ritual Special actions repeated in a strict order, often as part of a religious service.

sacred Having special importance in a religion.

scribe Someone who knows how to read or write, and who uses these skills in their work.

set-square Device for creating a RIGHT-ANGLE.

shaduf Water-lifting machine that has a bucket and a weight at opposite ends of a swinging arm.

shuttle Part of a LOOM holding thread, so that the WEAVER can pass it quickly over and under the WARP threads.

sledge Vehicle without wheels, that slides along the ground.

spell Special words repeated in a certain order to perform magic.

surveyor Someone who measures land or buildings, and makes maps.

till To turn over farmland so that crops grow.

triangle Flat shape that has three straight sides and three points.

warp Thread stretched tight between the ends of a LOOM; the WEAVER passes the SHUTTLE over and under alternate warp threads to make cloth.

weave To make cloth on a LOOM.

weaver Someone who WEAVES.

weft Thread that a WEAVER passes over and under WARP threads to make cloth on a LOOM.

WEBSITES

British Museum's ancient Egypt
www.ancientegypt.co.uk

An introduction to hieroglyphics
www.pbs.org/empires/egypt/special/hieroglyphs/introduction.html

Make a mummy game
www.bbc.co.uk/history/ancient/egyptians/launch_gms_mummy_maker.shtml

Pyramid challenge
www.bbc.co.uk/history/ancient/egyptians/launch_gms_pyramid_builder.shtml

INDEX